ALABAMA

The Heart of Dixie

BY
JOHN HAMILTON

Abdo & Daughters
An imprint of Abdo Publishing | abdopublishing.com

abdopublishing.com

Published by ABDO Publishing, a division of ABDO, PO Box 398166, Minneapolis, Minnesota 55439. Copyright © 2017 by Abdo Consulting Group, Inc. International copyrights reserved in all countries. No part of this book may be reproduced in any form without written permission from the publisher. ABDO & Daughters™ is a trademark and logo of ABDO Publishing.

Printed in the United States of America, North Mankato, Minnesota.
012016
092016

Editor: Sue Hamilton   **Contributing Editor:** Bridget O'Brien
Graphic Design: Sue Hamilton
Cover Art Direction: Candice Keimig   **Cover Photo Selection:** Neil Klinepier
Cover Photo: iStock
Interior Images: Alabama Department of Archives & History-Nathan Glick, Alabama Outlawz, Alamy, Amy Heatherington, AP, Birmingham Barons, Birmingham Blitz, Corbis, Getty, Glow Images, Granger Collection, Gunter Kuchler, HarperCollins (book covers), History in Full Color Restoration/Colorization, Huntsville Havoc, iStock, Library of Congress, Mercedes Alabama, Mile High Map, Mineral Information Institute, Mobile BayBears, Montgomery Biscuits, Mountain High Map, NASA, NOAA, One Mile Up, Rocket City United, U.S. Forest Service, U.S. Postal Service, University of New Brunswick, Walt Disney Pictures, Wark Photography.

Statistics: *State and City Populations*, U.S. Census Bureau, July 1, 2014 estimates; *Land and Water Area*, U.S. Census Bureau, 2010 Census, MAF/TIGER database; *State Temperature Extremes*, NOAA National Climatic Data Center; *Climatology and Average Annual Precipitation*, NOAA National Climatic Data Center, 1980-2015 statewide averages; *State Highest and Lowest Points*, NOAA National Geodetic Survey.

Websites: To learn more about the United States, visit booklinks.abdopublishing.com. These links are routinely monitored and updated to provide the most current information available.

Cataloging-in-Publication Data

Names: Hamilton, John, 1959- author.
Title: Alabama / by John Hamilton.
Description: Minneapolis, MN : Abdo Publishing, [2016] | The United States of
 America | Includes index.
Identifiers: LCCN 2015957502 | ISBN 9781680783032 (print) | ISBN
 9781680774078 (ebook)
Subjects: LCSH: Alabama--Juvenile literature.
Classification: DDC 976.1--dc23
LC record available at http://lccn.loc.gov/2015957502

CONTENTS

THE HEART OF DIXIE

Cotton

A labama is part of the Deep South. This southeastern region is often called Dixie. Alabama is a land brimming with civil rights history, Southern cooking, farms, and factories. It is also a place of natural beauty. The Appalachian Mountains are in the northeast. The warm waters of the Gulf of Mexico are along the state's southern shoreline. Outdoor lovers can explore forested mountains, deep caves, and hundreds of miles of inland waterways.

The U.S. Space & Rocket Center is in Huntsville, Alabama.

Farm products ruled Alabama's economy before the Civil War. Cotton was king. Most of it was harvested by African American slaves. Today, the state's farms share the spotlight with many other goods and services. They include medical research, iron and steel products, coal mines, and automobile factories. Alabama is even home to the nation's largest space research center.

*Little River Falls flows in Alabama's
Little River Canyon National Preserve.*

QUICK FACTS

Name: The word Alabama comes from the Native American Choctaw language. It probably means "clearers of the thicket" or "herb gatherers."

State Capital: Montgomery, population 200,481

Date of Statehood: December 14, 1819 (22nd state)

Population: 4,849,377 (23rd-most populous state)

Area (Total Land and Water): 52,420 square miles (135,767 sq km), 30th-largest state

Largest City: Birmingham, population 212,247

Nicknames: The Heart of Dixie; The Yellowhammer State; The Cotton State

Motto: "We Dare Defend Our Rights."

State Bird: Yellowhammer

State Flower: Camellia

State Rock: Marble

State Tree: Southern Longleaf Pine

State Song: "Alabama"

Highest Point: Mount Cheaha, in Talladega County, 2,413 feet (735 m)

Lowest Point: Gulf of Mexico, 0 feet (0 m)

Average July High Temperature: 91°F (33°C)

Record High Temperature: 112°F (44°C), in Centreville, on September 5, 1925

Average January Low Temperature: 34°F (1°C)

Record Low Temperature: -27°F (-33°C), in New Market, on January 30, 1966

Average Annual Precipitation: 56 inches (142 cm)

Number of U.S. Senators: 2

Number of U.S. Representatives: 7

U.S. Postal Service Abbreviation: AL

GEOGRAPHY

Alabama is located in the southeastern United States. This region is known as the Deep South. Alabama shares borders with four other states: Tennessee to the north, Georgia to the east, Mississippi to the west, and Florida to the south. A small portion of southwestern Alabama borders the Gulf of Mexico.

Alabama is the 30th-largest state, covering 52,420 square miles (135,767 sq km). It is shaped like a rectangle that is slightly smaller at the top. Low mountains dominate the north. They give way to plains that gradually descend toward the Gulf Coast. Many streams and rivers give Alabama a large inland waterway system.

A tugboat pushes goods down a winding river in Alabama.

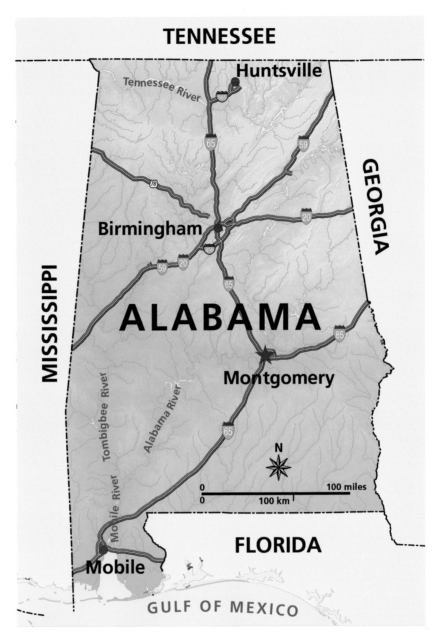

TENNESSEE

Tennessee River

Huntsville

65

59

78

Birmingham

20

59 20

65

ALABAMA

85

Montgomery

Tombigbee River

Alabama River

65

N

0   100 miles
0   100 km

Mobile River

FLORIDA

Mobile

GULF OF MEXICO

MISSISSIPPI

GEORGIA

Alabama's total land and water area is 52,420 square miles (135,767 sq km). It is the 30th-largest state. The state capital is Montgomery.

Noccalula Falls is in the forested highlands of northern Alabama.

Alabama has several natural regions. The northern part of Alabama includes forested highlands called the Appalachian Plateau. It is also known as the Cumberland Plateau. These low mountains contain thick forests and many waterfalls and canyons.

Southeast of the Cumberland Plateau is the Ridge and Valley region. Mountain ridges that run northeast to southwest are separated by miles of flatland. Southeast of this area is the Piedmont Upland region. Here, the mountains transform from high ridges into low, rolling foothills. While the southern Piedmont is relatively flat, the northern part contains some of the highest areas in the state. In this region is Mount Cheaha. It is Alabama's highest point. It rises 2,413 feet (735 m) above sea level.

The southern three-fifths of Alabama is called the East Gulf Coastal Plain. It is a flat, gentle plain that ends at the sandy beaches of the Gulf of Mexico. Wrapped around the midsection of this region is Alabama's "Black Belt." Its rich, black soil is ideal for farming. It was once home to many cotton plantations.

Alabama is crisscrossed by many rivers and streams. The most important include the Alabama, Tennessee, Tombigbee, Tensaw, and Mobile Rivers. Guntersville Lake is the largest body of water completely within the state.

Beneath Alabama's soil are thick layers of limestone, sandstone, and shale. In the mountainous parts of the state, water erosion has created many deep caves.

Natural Bridge is in the northwest part of Alabama. It is the longest natural bridge east of the Rocky Mountains. It measures 148 feet (45 m) long.

CLIMATE AND
WEATHER

Alabama's climate is subtropical. It has long, hot summers and mild winters. Temperatures are higher in the south because of warm, moist air from the Gulf of Mexico. Alabama summers are some of the hottest in the United States. The average July temperature statewide is 80°F (27°C), but daytime highs are usually well over 90°F (32°C). The average January temperature is a mild 45°F (7°C).

Alabama gets a lot of rain. It averages 56 inches (142 cm) of precipitation each year. The southern part of the state receives more rain than the north.

Because Alabama is near the warm coastal waters of the Gulf of Mexico, hurricanes sometimes bring fierce winds and flooding. In 2004, Hurricane Ivan battered the state with wind gusts of more than 90 miles per hour (145 kph). Frequent thunderstorms also strike Alabama. Severe thunderstorms sometimes spawn deadly tornadoes.

Lightning flashes during a thunderstorm in Birmingham, Alabama.

A tornado swirls through Tuscaloosa, Alabama. In April 2011, an outbreak of twisters killed at least 248 people.

PLANTS AND
ANIMALS

Alabama is one of the most ecologically diverse states in the country. It has many different kinds of landscapes. Cities and farms now occupy former woodlands, but forests continue to blanket about two-thirds of the state. The Sipsey Wilderness in northwestern Alabama is the largest protected forest in the state. It is a rugged area that includes dense stands of trees, ferns, waterfalls, and miles of hiking paths.

A hiker watches one of the many waterfalls found in Alabama's Sipsey Wilderness. The limestone and sandstone area is nicknamed "Land of 1,000 Waterfalls."

Trees surround Alabama's Lake Martin, one of the largest man-made lakes in the world.

Most of Alabama's forests are filled with pine trees. There are also large stands of oak, hickory, and maple trees. Other trees found in Alabama include poplar, cypress, gum, red cedar, southern white cedar, hemlock, hackberry, ash, and holly. Palm and palmetto trees grow in the warm coastal areas.

There are more than 300 kinds of wildflowers in Alabama. The oak-leaf hydrangea is the official state wildflower. Many other kinds of shrubs and flowering plants also grow in Alabama. These include mountain laurel, wisteria, and rhododendron. The official state flower is the camellia.

Oak-Leaf Hydrangea

Camellia

In 1999, the oak-leaf hydrangea and the camellia officially became Alabama's state wildflower and state flower.

PLANTS AND ANIMALS

The northern flicker, or yellowhammer woodpecker, is commonly seen in all parts of Alabama.

Because of Alabama's mild winters and many different habitats, the state has a rich diversity of birds, both native and migratory. Alabama's native birds include bald eagles, ospreys, hawks, quail, ducks, wild turkeys, geese, swans, herons, egrets, sandpipers, gulls, the Cape May warbler, and woodpeckers, including the northern flicker. The northern flicker is also known as the yellowhammer woodpecker. It is the official state bird. Alabama is the only state whose state bird is a woodpecker.

Pelicans sit on posts at Dauphin Island.

Large flocks of migratory birds can be found in the spring and fall in southern Alabama. They take refuge along the Gulf Coast at Dauphin Island and Bon Secour National Wildlife Refuge.

American alligators are found in the freshwater swamps of southern Alabama.

Alabama is home to a large variety of animals. White-tailed deer are found in great abundance. Also inhabiting Alabama's forests, but in far fewer numbers, are bears, panthers, and bobcats. Other members of Alabama's animal kingdom include bats, foxes, coyotes, raccoons, weasels, skunks, rabbits, opossums, and nine-banded armadillos. Alligators can be found lurking in the swamps of southern Alabama.

Largemouth Bass

Tarpon

More than 450 species of fish swim in Alabama's rivers, lakes, and reservoirs. They include sauger, gar, bluegill, sunfish, and catfish. The largemouth bass is Alabama's official state freshwater fish. Along the shores of the Gulf of Mexico, lucky anglers can catch Alabama shad and Gulf sturgeon. The state's official saltwater fish is the tarpon.

PLANTS AND ANIMALS

HISTORY

Centuries before Europeans colonized Alabama, Native Americans made the land their home. Some of the first were members of the Mississippian culture. They are often called the Mound

Alabama's Moundville Archaeological Park features displays and artifacts of Mound Builders.

Builders. They are famous for building large earthen hills 10 to 40 feet (3 to 12 m) high. Atop the mounds they placed houses, temples, and burial structures.

After the Mound Builders, several Native American tribes began settling in Alabama during the Middle Ages. They included the Creek, Cherokee, Alabama, Choctaw, and Chickasaw people. They lived mainly as farmers, potters, and traders.

Alonzo Álvarez de Pineda from Spain was probably the first European to see present-day Alabama. He came by way of the Gulf of Mexico, arriving by ship in 1519.

The 1540 Battle of Mabila remained the bloodiest conflict on American soil until the Civil War's Battle of Shiloh 332 years later. Hundreds, maybe thousands, of people died.

Another Spaniard, Hernando de Soto, crossed overland into Alabama in 1540. He led an expedition of more than 600 Spanish conquistadors who were exploring the American Southeast. They clashed with several Native American tribes. At the bloody Battle of Mabila against Chief Tuskaloosa, hundreds of conquistadors and Native Americans were killed. In later years, more Spanish soldiers arrived in Alabama, but their attempts to colonize the land failed.

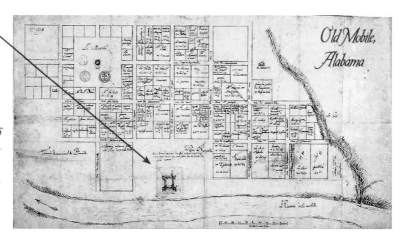

Fort Louis de la Louisiane was a square fort surrounded by a log palisade. It was built in 1702 and named for France's King Louis XIV.

Old Mobile, Alabama

More than 160 years after the Spanish first explored Alabama, French colonists in 1702 constructed a log fort called Fort Louis de la Louisiane. It was the first permanent European settlement of Alabama. It was located on the banks of the Mobile River about 30 miles (48 km) inland from a Gulf of Mexico inlet known today as Mobile Bay. Nine years later, the colony moved to the location of the present-day city of Mobile, Alabama, in 1711.

The French occupied the area for more than 60 years, until losing the Seven Years' War to Great Britain in 1763. After this time, the land changed hands several times during a tug-of-war between Great Britain, Spain, and the United States. Finally, the United States took control of Alabama in 1813. Just six years later, in 1819, Alabama became the 22nd state to join the Union.

Alabama's first capitol building was in Cahaba. After repeated floods, the state capital moved to Tuscaloosa in 1826. Centrally located, Montgomery became the permanent capital of Alabama in 1846.

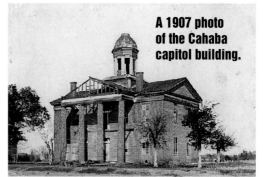

A 1907 photo of the Cahaba capitol building.

African Americans pick cotton on a plantation near Montgomery, Alabama, in the 1800s.

Settlers flooded into Alabama in the early 1800s. They were attracted by the state's climate and rich, black soil, which was perfect for growing cotton and other crops. African slaves were forced to work on huge farms called plantations.

The Indian Removal Act of 1830 drove most Alabama Native Americans off their lands as American expansion continued to push westward.

Jefferson Davis was sworn in as president of the Confederate states on February 18, 1861, in Montgomery, Alabama.

By the mid-1800s, the Northern states demanded that the South give up its slaves. The Southern states, including Alabama, refused. The plantations depended too much on slavery for their existence.

In 1861, Alabama seceded, or separated, from the United States. Alabama joined with other Southern states and formed the Confederate States of America. Montgomery, Alabama, became the first capital of the Confederacy (it was later moved to Richmond, Virginia).

The Civil War was fought from 1861 until 1865. Alabama troops were nicknamed "Yellowhammers" because the bright trim on their uniforms reminded people of the state bird, the northern flicker.

Confederate soldier reenactors fire a cannon at Alabama's Fort Blakeley. The Battle of Blakeley was the last major conflict of the Civil War. It took place two hours after Confederate General Lee surrendered to Union General Grant on April 9, 1865.

Left: Rosa Parks was arrested for refusing to give up her bus seat to a white person on December 1, 1955. Right: Parks sits in the front seat of a bus on December 21, 1956, after the U.S. Supreme Court declared bus segregation unconstitutional.

Alabama and the Confederacy lost the Civil War in 1865. For many long decades after the Civil War, former slaves and their African American descendants were badly mistreated. By the 1950s and 1960s, tension from racial discrimination boiled over, resulting in massive civil rights protests. Rosa Parks, Claudette Colvin, and others sparked the Montgomery bus boycott in 1955. Other protests occurred in the Alabama cities of Birmingham in 1963 and Selma in 1965. These protests brought about many positive changes for Americans in Alabama and across the country.

In recent years, Alabama has moved away from depending so much on farms. Instead, it has embraced high technology industries such as aerospace and auto manufacturing. Many Alabamians today have put their bitter past behind them and are working toward creating a land everyone can be proud of.

DID YOU KNOW?

- The first 911 emergency telephone system in the United States was set up in the town of Haleyville, Alabama, in 1968.

- Spring is tornado season for most states. However, Alabama has *two* tornado seasons. The first is in the spring. The second lasts from October through December. The state's tornadoes can be deadly. Twisters killed nearly 250 Alabamians during a severe weather outbreak in 2011.

- More than 80 million years ago, a huge meteorite at least 1,100 feet (335 m) wide struck the Earth, east of the modern-day town of Wetumpka, Alabama. The massive impact left a crater 4 miles (6.4 km) wide. The semi-circular ring of hills left over are still visible today.

- The *Black Pearl*, the sailing ship belonging to Captain Jack Sparrow in the Disney film *Pirates of the Caribbean: Dead Man's Chest*, was built at the Steiner Shipyard in Bayou La Batre, Alabama.

- Alabama is home to Space Camp and Space Academy, where kids can learn how to be astronauts and jet pilots. It is operated by the U.S. Space & Rocket Center in Huntsville, Alabama. More than 600,000 kids have been to Space Camp since it opened in 1982. Features and activities include computer flight simulators, Moon and Mars mission simulations, rocket construction and launch, and a space shuttle mock-up.

PEOPLE

Helen Keller (1880-1968) was only one year old when illness made her blind and deaf. She grew up to become a successful author, political activist, and speaker. She was the first deaf and blind

person to earn a bachelor of arts degree from an American college.

When she was a young girl, Keller learned a special sign language. Her teacher was Anne Sullivan. Sullivan spelled words in the palm of Keller's hand that symbolized everyday objects. Eventually, Keller understood the signing concept. From that point on she became an eager learner. During her lifetime, she wrote a total of 12 books and many magazine and newspaper articles.

Helen Keller was a fierce advocate for people with disabilities. Her story was made into a popular stage play and movie called *The Miracle Worker*. Keller was born in Tuscumbia, Alabama.

Nat King Cole (1919-1965) was one of America's most popular singers and entertainers during the 1940s and 1950s. His rich, baritone voice is remembered fondly by fans today, both young and old.

Cole started his career in the 1930s playing jazz piano. His songwriting appealed to a wide audience. Many of his compositions influenced rock performers who came later, such as Bo Diddley. His most famous tunes included "The Christmas Song," "Mona Lisa," and "Unforgettable."

Cole starred in *The Nat King Cole Show* on NBC from 1956 to 1957, becoming the first African American to host a network TV variety show. Cole was born in Montgomery, Alabama.

Jesse Owens (1913-1980) was a track-and-field star who won four gold medals at the 1936 Summer Olympic Games in Berlin, Germany. Nazi German dictator Adolf Hitler had boasted that black men were inferior to white German athletes. Owens made Hitler look foolish. Many sports fans consider Owens one of the greatest athletes of the 20th century.

Owens was often sick as a child. Through much practice and encouragement by his coaches, he grew into a world-class athlete. He broke many track-and-field records in high school. At Ohio State University, he was known as the "Buckeye Bullet." During a Big Ten meet in 1935, he broke three world records and tied a fourth in only 45 minutes.

When asked the secret of his success, Owens once said, "I let my feet spend as little time on the ground as possible." Jesse Owens was born near the town of Oakville, Alabama.

Harper Lee (1926-2016) wrote the classic national bestseller *To Kill a Mockingbird.* It won a Pulitzer Prize in 1961, and was turned into an Oscar-winning movie. The book is about six-year-old Scout Finch and her lawyer father, Atticus, who live in a small town in Alabama. Atticus defends an African American man who is falsely accused of a terrible crime.

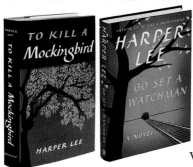

To Kill a Mockingbird deals with serious issues, such as crime and racial discrimination in the South. The author has said she did not expect the book to be published, and was surprised at its success. People love Lee's writing for its humor, warmth, and depiction of justice and morality. *Go Set a Watchman*, another Lee book with Atticus Finch and an adult Scout, was published in 2015. Harper Lee was born and raised in Monroeville, Alabama.

CITIES

Birmingham is the largest city in Alabama. It has a population of 212,247. Located in the north-central part of the state, its nickname is the "Pittsburgh of the South." Since its founding in 1871, Birmingham for many years was a center of iron and steel production. The city's industrial strength helped transform Alabama from a farm state into a manufacturing powerhouse. Although manufacturing isn't as important today, Birmingham remains one of the strongest centers of commerce in the Southeast. Important industries include banking, medical care, and insurance. The city is also the location of the University of Alabama School of Medicine and the University of Alabama at Birmingham.

Montgomery is the capital of Alabama. It has a population of 200,481, and is the second-largest city in the state. It is located in the center of Alabama's southern half, along the shores of the Alabama River. Once the first capital of the Confederacy during the Civil War, Montgomery was the birthplace of the modern civil rights movement in the 1950s and 1960s. Today, many government workers make their home in Montgomery. The city also attracts high-tech manufacturing, hosts many cultural events, and is home to Alabama State University. Montgomery has a newly revitalized downtown area. The city also recognizes its past, hosting the acclaimed Civil Rights Memorial and the Rosa Parks Library and Museum.

Mobile is the third-largest city in Alabama. It has a population of 194,675. It is situated at the end of Mobile Bay along the Gulf of Mexico. Known as "The Port City," it has the state's only saltwater port. Shipbuilding is an important industry. Mobile is also a center for aerospace, steel processing, medicine, and construction. The city's annual Carnival celebration is the oldest in the country. It got its start more than 300 years ago, in 1703.

Huntsville has a population of 188,226. It is Alabama's fourth-largest city. It is located in the north-central part of the state. The city was founded in 1805 as a center for the cotton and railroad industries. After World War II, these businesses gave way to aerospace with the addition of the U.S. Army's Redstone Arsenal and NASA's Marshall Space Flight Center. The facility has planned and supported many United States space missions, including the Apollo missions to the Moon and flights to the International Space Station. Because aerospace is so important to its economy, Huntsville is nicknamed "The Rocket City."

TRANSPORTATION

The Port of Mobile is Alabama's only saltwater port. It is one of the largest seaports in the nation. It has easy access to the Gulf of Mexico and inland ports by way of Alabama's huge system of rivers and canals. The state has the second-largest inland waterway system in the country. It is used to transport raw materials and finished goods by barges and other ships. Ships cruising through Alabama can stop at three major ports on the Tennessee River, two ports on the man-made Tennessee-Tombigbee Waterway, and one port on the Alabama River. The Tenn-Tom Waterway connects Alabama to a system of more than 15,000 miles (24,140 km) of waterways in 23 states.

Ships move goods up the Tennessee-Tombigbee Waterway.

A plane takes off from Birmingham-Shuttlesworth International Airport.

There are six major commercial airports in Alabama. The busiest is Birmingham-Shuttlesworth International Airport. In 2013, it handled air travel for more than 2.6 million passengers.

Alabama is crisscrossed by about 4,000 miles (6,437 km) of rail lines. In 2011, freight trains hauled more than 162 million tons (147 million metric tons) of products through or within the state. Coal accounts for about a third of the rail traffic. Other products include grain, lumber, chemicals, and metal products.

Automobiles and trucks travel on more than 101,837 miles (163,891 km) of public roads in Alabama. There are five major interstate highways that cross the state. A sixth is under construction.

Traffic flows on an interstate highway in Huntsville, Alabama.

NATURAL
RESOURCES

About 23 million acres (9.3 million ha) of Alabama, or 70 percent of the state, is covered by forests. Commercial logging in the north produces lumber for building materials and paper products.

Alabama has abundant water resources. Many rivers are used to transport goods or generate hydroelectric power.

Alabama coal fields are important to the state's economy. The steel mills in the Birmingham area were built because of the nearby coal fields. Other minerals mined include limestone, dolomite, granite, sandstone, and quartzite. Sand, gravel, and crushed stone are also important natural resources.

Pine logs are loaded onto a truck at a logging site outside of Citronelle, Alabama.

A large chicken farm in Monroe County, Alabama.

About one-fourth of Alabama's land is used for farming. The state's climate and rich variety of soil make it a great place to raise livestock and grow crops. The most important agricultural product is poultry. Others include cattle, peanuts, corn, and soybeans. Alabama is still called "The Cotton State," but cotton is much less vital today to the state's economy.

Outdoor recreation is a big moneymaker for Alabama. The commercial fishing industry is also important. Fleets of boats ply the waters of the Gulf of Mexico. They bring back valuable hauls of red snapper, mackerel, and shellfish.

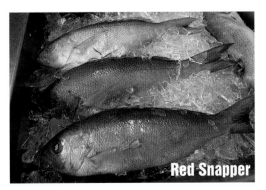
Red Snapper

NATURAL RESOURCES

INDUSTRY

Alabama was once well known for its agricultural goods, especially cotton. In modern times, the state has become a manufacturing powerhouse. Much of Alabama's economic growth in the past 20 years has been because of car manufacturing. Large automobile factories in the state include those run by Honda, Hyundai, Mercedes-Benz, and Toyota. Alabama factories also produce chemicals, plastics, electronics, computer hardware, textiles, and parts for jets and rockets.

Sparks fly as robots weld vehicle frames on an assembly line at the Honda Manufacturing of Alabama facility in Lincoln, Alabama.

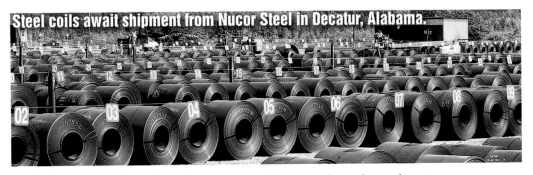
Steel coils await shipment from Nucor Steel in Decatur, Alabama.

Alabama has long been a center of iron and steel production. Thousands of Alabamians are employed by major steel companies, including ThyssenKrupp, Nucor, and U.S. Steel.

Restaurants and supermarkets are plentiful in Alabama, as well as many other kinds of retail stores and shops. Also important are service industries such as accounting, banking, legal, and repair shops. Construction, health care, and tourism are also key industries. About 20 million tourists visit Alabama each year, amounting to more than $8 billion in spending and employing more than 160,000 people.

There are nearly 300 aerospace and defense companies that operate in Alabama. Many are located in the Huntsville area, home to NASA's Marshall Space Flight Center. Major aerospace companies in Alabama include Airbus, Northrop Grumman, Boeing, Sikorsky, Lockheed Martin, and Bell Helicopter.

Boeing workers load a Delta IV rocket onto a ship in Decatur, Alabama.

SPORTS

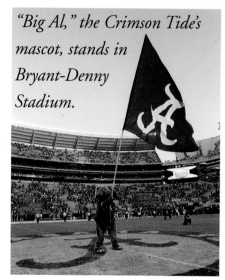

"Big Al," the Crimson Tide's mascot, stands in Bryant-Denny Stadium.

College football is big in Alabama. The most popular teams are from the University of Alabama in Tuscaloosa, and Auburn University in Auburn, Alabama. The University of Alabama's Crimson Tide plays in Bryant-Denny Stadium, one of the largest stadiums in America. It seats nearly 102,000 fans. It is partly named after legendary head coach Paul "Bear" Bryant. During a career that spanned 25 years, he won a record 323 games, including 15 bowl victories and 6 national championships.

There are no major league professional sports teams in Alabama, but there are several minor league clubs. Some of the most popular include the Birmingham Barons (baseball), the Montgomery Biscuits (baseball), the Mobile BayBears (baseball), the Birmingham Blitz (basketball), the Alabama Outlawz (indoor football), the Huntsville Havoc (hockey), and Rocket City United (soccer).

Many Alabamians love stock car racing. The most famous racetrack is the Talladega Superspeedway motorsports complex in Talladega, Alabama. NASCAR hosts several events here, including the Sprint Cup Series. Known for its steep banking, the challenging tri-oval track has a length of 2.66 miles (4.3 km). The stadium seats nearly 80,000 race fans.

ENTERTAINMENT

The Alabama Shakespeare Festival in Montgomery is one of the largest Shakespeare festivals in the world. More than 300,000 people come to see the many plays the festival produces each year.

For lovers of fine music, there are symphony orchestras in Birmingham, Huntsville, Mobile, and Tuscaloosa. The Alabama Symphony Orchestra in Birmingham is one of the nation's top professional orchestras.

Alabama has many museums scattered across the state. The U.S. Space & Rocket Center in Huntsville contains a vast collection of manned space flight hardware. More than 16 million people have toured the center since it opened its doors in 1970. In Mobile, the battleship USS *Alabama* has been turned into a floating museum. Famous for its combat role during World War II, the ship now rests in Mobile Bay's Battleship Memorial Park.

Battleship Memorial Park is a popular military park and museum in Mobile, Alabama.

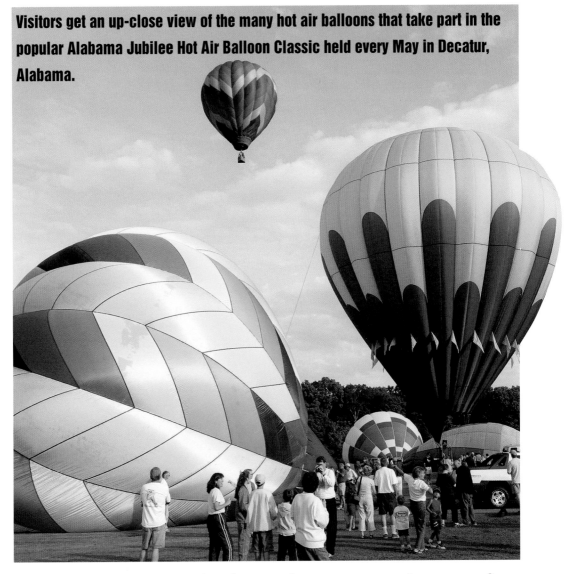

Visitors get an up-close view of the many hot air balloons that take part in the popular Alabama Jubilee Hot Air Balloon Classic held every May in Decatur, Alabama.

Each Memorial Day weekend, more than 50,000 people turn out for the Alabama Jubilee Hot Air Balloon Classic in Decatur, Alabama. As many as 60 balloons take flight during the festival.

Quieter activities in Alabama include browsing through the more than eight million books contained in the state's libraries, or even simply taking a hike through the fern-draped forest of the Sipsey Wilderness or other popular outdoor destinations.

TIMELINE

700—The earliest people in Alabama begin building ceremonial mounds.

1400—Creek, Cherokee, and other Native American tribes begin settling in Alabama.

Hernando de Soto

1519—Spain begins exploration of Alabama. Five attempts at colonization fail.

1682—France begins exploring Alabama.

1702—France builds Europe's first successful settlement in Alabama.

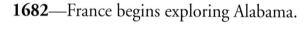

1819—Alabama admitted as the 22nd state in the Union.

1820s—Settlers flood into Alabama. Many cotton plantations are started.

1861—Alabama joins the Confederacy to keep slavery legal. The Civil War begins.

1865—The Confederacy is defeated in the Civil War. All slaves are set free. Alabama is brought back into the Union three years later in 1868.

1871—The city of Birmingham is founded. "The Magic City" becomes a center for iron and steel production.

1950s—The civil rights movement to give blacks full equality begins and gathers strength.

1960s—Blacks win full legal equality with whites. Alabama becomes a center for United States missions into space.

1970s until Today—Aerospace and other modern industries continue to boost Alabama's economy. Large automakers and aircraft manufacturers build factories in the state, creating many new jobs.

2016—The University of Alabama football team wins its fourth national championship in seven years. The Crimson Tide finished its 2015 regular season with a 14-1 record.

GLOSSARY

CIVIL RIGHTS MOVEMENT

A nationwide effort beginning in the 1950s to reform federal and state laws so that African Americans could enjoy full equality.

CIVIL WAR

The war fought between America's Northern and Southern states from 1861-1865. The Southern states were for slavery. They wanted to start their own country. Northern states fought against slavery and a division of the country.

CONFEDERACY

The Southern states of Alabama, Arkansas, Florida, Georgia, Louisiana, Mississippi, North Carolina, South Carolina, Tennessee, Texas, and Virginia. These states wanted to keep slavery legal. They broke away from the United States during the Civil War and formed their own country, known as the Confederate States of America, or the Confederacy. The Confederacy ended in 1865 when the war ended and the 11 Confederate states rejoined the United States.

DIXIE

A nickname for the southern region of the United States. It may have started with the drawing of boundaries between Pennsylvania and Maryland in the 1760s. The line between those colonies was created by surveyors Charles Mason and Jeremiah Dixon. It became known as the Mason-Dixon Line. People soon after began joking that everything north of that line was Mason country and everything south of it was Dixon. Dixon eventually became Dixie.

MIDDLE AGES
In European history, the Middle Ages were a period defined by historians as roughly between 476 AD and 1450 AD.

NATIONAL AERONAUTICS AND SPACE ADMINISTRATION (NASA)
A United States government agency started in 1958. NASA's goals include space exploration, as well as increasing people's understanding of Earth, our solar system, and the universe.

PLAIN
A large, flat area of land, often filled with grasses, but with few trees.

PLANTATION
A large farm where crops such as tobacco, sugar cane, and cotton are grown. Workers usually live right on the property. Early plantation owners in North America used cheap slave labor to make their operations more profitable.

PLATEAU
A large, flat section of land that is raised up from the surrounding countryside.

SECEDE
To withdraw membership in a union or alliance.

UNION
The Northern states united against the Confederacy. "Union" also refers to all of the states of the United States. President Lincoln wanted to preserve the Union, keeping the Northern and Southern states together.

WATERWAY
A stream or river wide and deep enough for boats to travel along.

INDEX